YOU
MAKE ME
PROUD

summersdale

YOU MAKE ME PROUD

Summersdale Publishers Ltd
46 West Street
Chichester
West Sussex
PO19 1RP
UK

www.summersdale.com

Printed and bound in the Czech Republic

ISBN: 978-1-78685-053-9

Substantial discounts on bulk quantities of Summersdale books are available to corporations, professional associations and other organisations. For details contact general enquiries: telephone: +44 (0) 1243 771107, fax: +44 (0) 1243 786300 or email: enquiries@summersdale.com.

To be yourself in a world that is constantly trying to make you something else is the greatest accomplishment.

RALPH WALDO EMERSON

Mastering others
is strength.
Mastering yourself
is true power.

LAO TZU

With ordinary talent
and extraordinary
perseverance,
all things are
attainable.

THOMAS FOWELL BUXTON

The roughest road often leads to the top.

CHRISTINA AGUILERA

Difficulties are things that
show a person what they are.

EPICTETUS

We don't even know
how strong we are
until we are forced
to bring that hidden
strength forward.

ISABEL ALLENDE

YOU'VE COME SO
FAR FROM WHERE
YOU STARTED.

Believe you can and you're halfway there.

THEODORE ROOSEVELT

YOU ARE SO STRONG.

Optimism is essential to achievement and it is also the foundation of courage.

NICHOLAS MURRAY BUTLER

Great works are performed, not by strength, but by perseverance.

SAMUEL JOHNSON

YOU DESERVE EVERY SUCCESS.

The world you desire can be won. It exists... it is real... it is possible... it's yours.

AYN RAND

The more we do, the more we can do.

WILLIAM HAZLITT

You can't stop the waves, but you can learn to surf.

JON KABAT-ZINN

YOU ARE THE CREATOR OF YOUR FUTURE.

It always seems impossible
until it's done.

NELSON MANDELA

If you think you are too small to make a difference, try sleeping with a mosquito.

DALAI LAMA

To accomplish great things, we must not only act, but also dream; not only plan but also believe.

ANATOLE FRANCE

THERE'S NOTHING YOU CAN'T DO.

Don't let what you cannot do interfere with what you can do.

JOHN R. WOODEN

YOU
ARE
AMAZING!

Success is the sum of small efforts, repeated day in and day out.

ROBERT COLLIER

BE PROUD OF
WHO YOU ARE
AND ALL YOU'VE
OVERCOME.

What we see depends mainly on what we look for.

JOHN LUBBOCK

Every man is the architect
of his own fortune.

APPIUS CLAUDIUS CAECUS

Act as if what
you do makes a
difference. It does.

WILLIAM JAMES

Plunge boldly into the thick of life, and seize it where you will, it is always interesting.

JOHANN WOLFGANG VON GOETHE

If you are going through
hell, keep going.

WINSTON CHURCHILL

Those who wish to sing, always find a song.

SWEDISH PROVERB

YOU ARE
SIGNIFICANT.

Perseverance is
stubbornness with
a purpose.

JOSH SHIPP

Wheresoever you go, go with all your heart.

CONFUCIUS

TAKE PRIDE IN HOW FAR YOU'VE COME.

Achievement is not always success... It is honest endeavour, persistent effort to do the best possible under any and all circumstances.

ORISON SWETT MARDEN

You are never too old
to set a new goal or
dream a new dream.

LES BROWN

You gain strength, courage, and confidence by every experience in which you really stop to look fear in the face.

ELEANOR ROOSEVELT

Obstacles are the raw materials of great accomplishment.

TOMMY NEWBERRY

Always act like you're wearing an invisible crown.

ANONYMOUS

YOU ARE
IN CONTROL OF
YOUR OWN LIFE.

If we all did the things we are capable of, we would literally astound ourselves.

THOMAS EDISON

Turn your face towards the sun and the shadows will fall behind you.

MAORI PROVERB

When patterns
are broken, new
worlds emerge.

TULI KEPFERBERG

The secret of getting
ahead is getting started.

MARK TWAIN

BELIEVE IN HOW FAR YOU CAN GO.

Don't let them tame you.

ISADORA DUNCAN

Just be yourself, there is no one better.

TAYLOR SWIFT

Just say yes, just
say there's nothing
holding you back.

ZOELLA

Every day may not be good, but there's something good in every day.

ALICE MORSE EARLE

HAVE FAITH
IN YOURSELF.

If you're going to
doubt something,
doubt your
own limits.

DON WARD

Who seeks, shall find.

SOPHOCLES

I'm convinced that about half of what separates successful entrepreneurs from the non-successful is perseverance.

STEVE JOBS

Every strike brings me closer to the next home run.

BABE RUTH

PROVE

THEM

WRONG!

One may walk over the highest mountain one step at a time.

JOHN WANAMAKER

**Dare to love yourself
as if you were a
rainbow with gold
at both ends.**

ABERJHANI

IT TAKES COURAGE TO BE YOURSELF.

Be yourself. The world
worships the original.

INGRID BERGMAN

Champions keep playing until they get it right.

BILLY JEAN KING

The difference between perseverance and obstinacy is that one comes from a strong will and the other from a strong wont.

HENRY WARD BEECHER

Nobody can do everything, but everyone can do something.

ANONYMOUS

DO WHAT YOU THINK YOU CANNOT DO.

Don't go through life,
grow through life.

ERIC BUTTERWORTH

The potential for greatness lives within each of us.

WILMA RUDOLPH

Trust yourself. You know
more than you think you do.

BENJAMIN SPOCK

The best way out is
always through.

ROBERT FROST

KEEP

GOING.

Nothing is impossible.
The word itself says
'I'm possible'!

AUDREY HEPBURN

A strong, positive self-image is the best possible preparation for success.

JOYCE BROTHERS

Perseverance is not a long race; it is many short races one after the other.

WALTER ELLIOT

It's kind of fun to do
the impossible.

WALT DISNEY

I am a slow walker, but I never walk back.

ABRAHAM LINCOLN

What lies behind you and what lies in front of you, pales in comparison to what lies inside of you.

RALPH WALDO EMERSON

YOU DESERVE
TO BE PROUD
OF YOURSELF.

Run your own race of life, with a single-minded vision of purpose.

LAILAH GIFTY AKITA

It's always too early to quit.

NORMAN VINCENT PEALE

OWN WHO

YOU ARE.

"

There is only one
map to the journey
of life and it lives
within your heart.

WILLIE NELSON

Integrity has no
need of rules.

ALBERT CAMUS

The worst enemy
to creativity is
self-doubt.

SYLVIA PLATH

WHAT YOU DO MAKES A DIFFERENCE.

Opportunities multiply
as they are seized.

SUN TZU

The will to persevere is often the difference between failure and success.

DAVID SARNOFF

For myself I am an optimist –
it does not seem to be much
use being anything else.

WINSTON CHURCHILL

BELIEVE YOU CAN, AND YOU WILL.

You don't get harmony when everybody sings the same note.

ANONYMOUS

When everything
seems to be going
against you,
remember that the
airplane takes off
against the wind.

HENRY FORD

Dare to be different and
to set your own pattern,
live your own life and
follow your own star.

_____

WILFERD PETERSON

TURN YOUR DREAMS INTO PLANS.

The best way to
predict your future
is to create it.

ABRAHAM LINCOLN

If you can imagine it,
you can achieve it.
If you can dream it,
you can become it.

WILLIAM ARTHUR WARD

Your time is limited, so don't waste it living someone else's life.

STEVE JOBS

YOU WILL

GET

THERE.

No one succeeds
without effort... Those
who succeed owe their
success to perseverance.

RAMANA MAHARSHI

Your soul is all that you possess. Take it in hand and make something of it!

MARTIN H. FISCHER

**First, think.
Second, believe.
Third, dream.
And finally, dare.**

WALT DISNEY

POSITIVITY IS CONTAGIOUS!

Don't count the days,
make the days count.

MUHAMMAD ALI

In the middle of difficulty lies opportunity.

ALBERT EINSTEIN

Don't give up.
Don't lose hope.
Don't sell out.

CHRISTOPHER REEVE

Success is only meaningful and enjoyable if it feels like your own.

MICHELLE OBAMA

TRUST
YOURSELF.

**It does not matter
how slowly you
go, so long as
you do not stop.**

CONFUCIUS

We have to dare
to be ourselves,
however frightening
or strange that self
may prove to be.

MAY SARTON

If you fell
down yesterday,
stand up today.

H. G. WELLS

Let perseverance be your
engine and hope your fuel.

H. JACKSON BROWN JR

STARS CAN'T SHINE WITHOUT DARKNESS.

We may encounter
many defeats but we
must not be defeated.

MAYA ANGELOU

If opportunity doesn't knock, build a door.

MILTON BERLE

These are the days that must happen to you.

WALT WHITMAN

Anything you really want, you can attain, if you really go after it.

WAYNE DYER

THIS DAY IS YOURS.

Just throw away all thoughts of imaginary things, and stand firm in that which you are.

KABIR

Sometimes you gotta create what you want to be a part of.

GERI WEITZMAN

It all begins and ends in your mind. What you give power to has power over you, if you allow it.

LEON BROWN

HAVE THE COURAGE OF YOUR CONVICTIONS.

What progress, you ask,
have I made? I have begun
to be a friend to myself.

HECATO

What I am is good enough if I would only be it openly.

CARL ROGERS

You are perfectly cast in your life. I can't imagine anyone but you in the role. Go play.

LIN-MANUEL MIRANDA

YOU HAVE THE POWER TO CREATE CHANGE.

Difficult roads often lead to beautiful destinations.

MELCHOR LIM

Only in the darkness can you see the stars.

MARTIN LUTHER KING JR

Courage is being
scared to death but
saddling up anyway.

JOHN WAYNE

YOU HAVE EVERYTHING YOU NEED.

The final forming
of a person's
character lies in
their own hands.

ANNE FRANK

Follow your honest convictions, and stay strong.

WILLIAM MAKEPEACE THACKERAY

Remember, if you ever
need a helping hand, it's
at the end of your arm.

SAM LEVENSON

IT'S NEVER TOO LATE.

Everything you've
ever wanted
is on the other
side of fear.

GEORGE ADDAIR

There is just one life for
each of us: our own.

EURIPIDES

NEVER
GIVE UP.

There is no magic to achievement. It's really about hard work, choices, and persistence.

MICHELLE OBAMA

The harder the conflict, the more glorious the triumph.

THOMAS PAINE

You have to
be unique and
different and shine
in your own way.

LADY GAGA

KEEP YOUR
HEAD UP.

Life is a pure flame, and we live by an invisible sun within us.

THOMAS BROWNE

Do what you can
with what you have,
where you are.

THEODORE ROOSEVELT

STAY

STRONG.

Fortune favours
the bold.

LATIN PROVERB

It takes courage to grow up and become who you really are.

E. E. CUMMINGS

Your attitude, not your aptitude, will determine your altitude.

ZIG ZIGLAR

Things work out best for those who make the best of the way things work out.

ANONYMOUS

WHEN YOU
CAN'T SING, HUM.

Just when the caterpillar thought the world was over, it became a butterfly.

ANONYMOUS

Every day brings a chance for you to draw in a breath, kick off your shoes... and dance.

OPRAH WINFREY

What we do flows from who we are.

PAUL VITALE

YOU CAN DO IT;
ALL YOU HAVE
TO DO IS TRY.

Respect yourself and others will respect you.

CONFUCIUS

Do your little bit of good where you are; it's those little bits of good put together that overwhelm the world.

DESMOND TUTU

YOU ARE
CAPABLE OF
AMAZING THINGS.

Follow your own star.

DANTE ALIGHIERI

Accept no one's definition of your life; define yourself.

HARVEY FIERSTEIN

DON'T TELL PEOPLE YOUR DREAMS. SHOW THEM.

"

Make the most of yourself by fanning the tiny, inner sparks of possibility into flames of achievement.

GOLDA MEIR

When you're true to who you are, amazing things happen.

DEBORAH NORVILLE

"

If you're interested in finding out more about our books, find us on Facebook at **Summersdale Publishers** and follow us on Twitter at **@Summersdale**.

www.summersdale.com